£50
75p
30p
C

FOLK TOYS
and how to make them

Warren Farnworth
Illustrated by Elizabeth Haines

A Chatto Activity Book

Chatto and Windus

Published by Chatto and Windus Ltd.
42 William IV Street, London WC2N 4DF

Clarke, Irwin and Co. Ltd., Toronto

Other Chatto Activity Books
SHADOWS IN COLOUR
TABLETOP THEATRES
PRESSING FLOWERS AND LEAVES

Text © Warren Farnworth 1974
Illustrations © Chatto & Windus Ltd 1974
ISBN 0 7011 5054 8

Printed in Great Britain by
T. & A. Constable Ltd., Edinburgh

Contents

Introduction

It must have been a girl or boy who invented the first toy. A little girl imagining a knobbly branch of wood as a doll, or shaking a dried gourd full of seeds for a rattle. A small boy whistling through a blade of grass, or kicking a rounded pebble with his friends.

And it must have been a long, long time ago—when we dressed in skins and lived in fear of the tiger and the bear.

Nowadays you can walk into a toy shop and buy almost anything—from a simple rubber ball to a computerised, space-age robot.

This book has no computerised robots—but toys which you can make for yourself. Some, like the Egyptian clapper, are thousands of years old. Others, like the thaumatrope (and you must turn to page 6 to find out what that is) are quite young.

But to make a clapper is to hear an echo of what Egyptian children must have heard five thousand years ago on the banks of the Nile—and to spin a thaumatrope is to see what your great grandmother might have seen when Queen Victoria was on the throne.

And there are many others. Toys from every land. All of them are quite simple to make—and very cheap. Some have a story to tell—others have stories long forgotten. Just turn the pages and see.

Porotiti
New Zealand

This is the song which a Maori boy or girl might sing to the sound of a spinning porotiti:

Ka kukume,
Ka kukume au i te tau o taku porotiti
Ki whakaawe ki Rangi-taiki
Ka hoki mai te tau o taku porotiti
Hu—hu, wheo—wheo.

This is what it means:

I pull, I pull the cord of my porotiti,
to far-off Rangi-taiki.
The cord of my porotiti now reverses;
Hu—hu, wheo—wheo

Porotitis (funny name) seem to have been made everywhere. The Maoris of New Zealand make them from the heart of the kaiwhiria tree (whatever that is); the Japanese from bamboo (they call them 'bun-buns'); and the Eskimos from ivory (they call them 'buzzes'); but you can make one from almost anything.

Materials you will need:
▶A piece of thick cardboard and a metre length of string. The shape of the cardboard doesn't seem to matter, but try a round piece first, cut to the size of a coffee jar top.
Pierce two holes in the centre; thread the string through and tie a knot, as you see here.

To spin the porotiti, hold it loosely with your index fingers through the loops at either end, and spin it round until the string becomes tightly twisted—pull the string taut, and the cardboard will spin even faster. With practice, by tautening and slackening the string, you can keep the cardboard spinning—first one way, then the other—for hours on end; or pass it (still spinning) to someone else.

Try out lots of different shapes and sizes of cardboard, different lengths of string, and different hole positions to see which ones work the best.
You can also try using a tin lid, a large button, or carve a porotiti from a piece of wood.
To make it even better, paint or colour your porotiti with different colours and shapes.

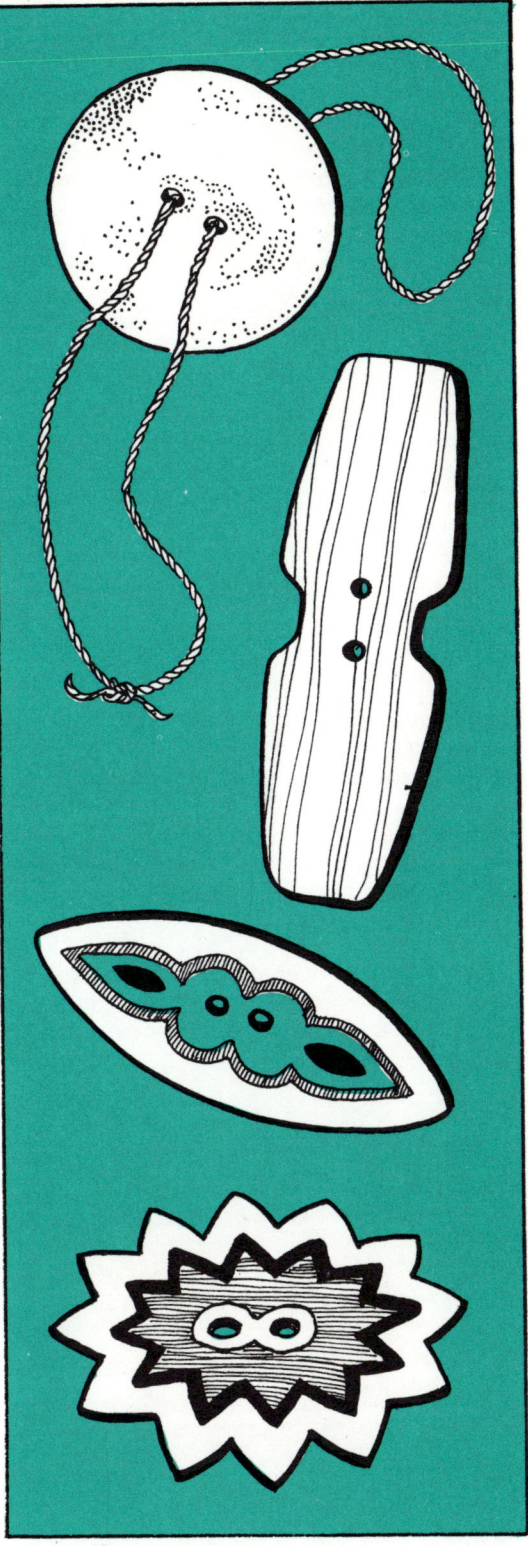

Thaumatrope
British Isles

The word 'thaumatrope' comes from two Greek words, 'thauma' meaning wonder, and 'tropos' meaning turning. Put them together and you have 'turning wonder'. Dr. John Ayrton Paris invented the thaumatrope in 1825, and it was soon to become a very popular toy, not only with British children, but with children all over the world.

Materials you will need:
▶A small piece of cardboard—circular or square, and two short lengths of thread.

What to do:

1. Make two holes in the cardboard, and fasten a loop of thread through each hole, as shown.

2. On one side of the cardboard, draw a bird—and on the other an *upside-down* cage.

3. Now, hold the toy loosely with your index fingers through the loops at either end. Spin it round until the thread becomes tightly twisted—pull the thread taut and see what happens. First you see the bird, then the cage—then the bird—then the cage. But it all happens so quickly that what you really see is a bird in a cage.

Of course, your thaumatrope doesn't have to be a bird in a cage—it could be all kinds of things. Some other ideas are shown here; can you think of any more?

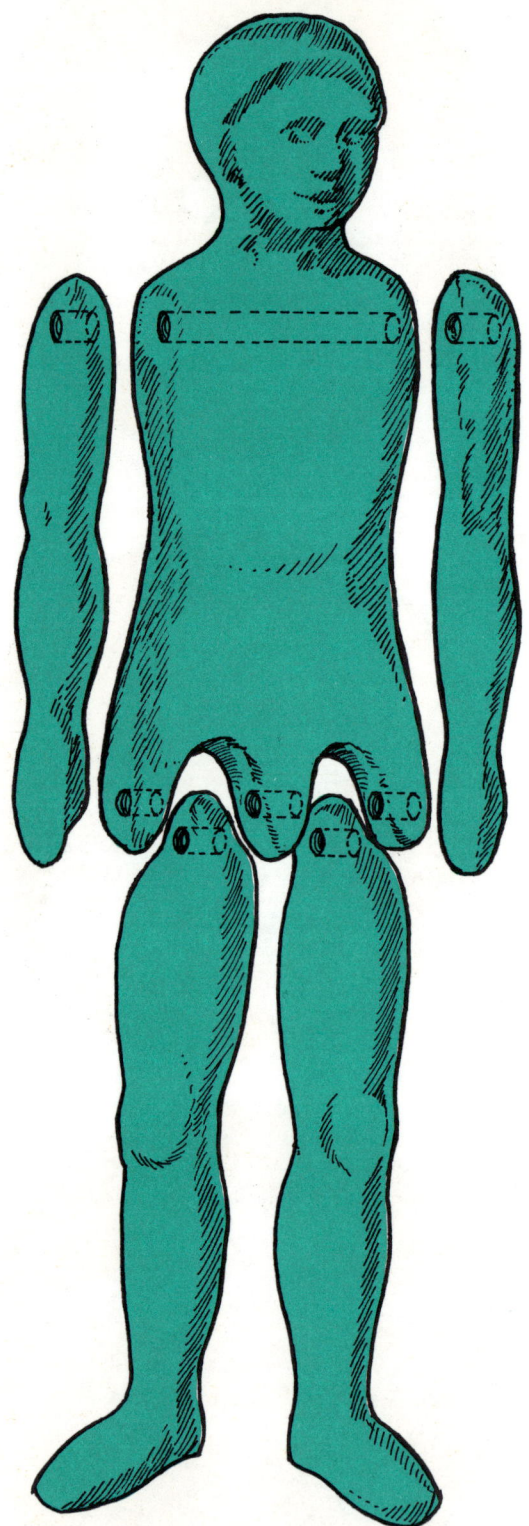

Jointed Doll
Greece

The small jointed doll opposite comes from Greece. It is made from fired clay, and is more than two thousand years old.

Materials you will need:

▶Some modelling paste (see page 48) and a few short lengths of strong twine or thin string.

What to do:

1. Model the body, first of all, something like this. It doesn't matter what shape or size it is, but if this is your first attempt, keep the body fairly small and simple.

2. Before the paste hardens, make holes (large enough for the string to pass through) at the shoulders (passing right through the body) and at the pelvis, as shown.

3. Now the arms and legs—two of each, of course. Make them in proportion to the body —keep them simple (fingers and toes can be painted on afterwards)—and don't forget to put in the holes.

4. When the modelling paste has hardened, fasten the pieces together with string.

One of the Greek dolls shown here is carrying castanets. She may be a dancer. But your dolls can be anything or anybody—and you can paint them or dress them in any way you want.

Bear and Blacksmith
Russia

Many are the stories told about the bear. He is wise, fierce, intelligent and strong. In olden days, people used to worship him, especially those who lived in the forests of northern Europe and Asia. They believed that he had magical powers, and that he could understand the speech of humans.

How he met the blacksmith, or why, is a mystery. Perhaps they just met in the forest, and—rather than fight—decided to have a trial of strength. Whatever it was, this is what the toy seems to represent.

The traditional Russian toy is usually carved from soft wood, and sold (very cheaply) at local fairs and markets. If you are clever with your hands, you can make a wooden one for yourself from pieces of ply-wood cut with a fretsaw, but to begin with, here is a cardboard version which everyone can make.

Materials you will need:
▶Cardboard and paper-fasteners.

What to do:

1. Cut out the shapes of the bear and the blacksmith from thick cardboard, making holes at A, B, C, and D. You may find it easier to make a tracing of them first, but whatever you do, take care to position the holes exactly as you see them here.

2. Cut out two cardboard strips, each one 30 cm long by 2½ cm wide, making holes at E, F, G, and H.

3. Fasten the four pieces together with brass paper fasteners—A to E, B to G, C to F, and D to H, and paint or colour the model in any way you wish.

10

4. By holding the model at Y, and pushing X in and out, the bear and the blacksmith will hammer away in turn. Although the bear and the blacksmith (sometimes a wood-chopper) is a traditional Russian toy, many other countries have invented versions of their own. Sometimes the figures represent birds pecking at seed, animals drinking at a pool, two people washing clothes in a tub, a man trying to pull a lazy donkey, or even two boxers boxing.

Can you think of anything else?

Windmill
Holland

The windmill toy has been a favourite of European children for many hundreds of years. The earliest ones—made in Holland—were very simple, just two cross-pieces of wood nailed to a stick. Later, paper and tin were used, and modern seaside ones are now made from plastic.

Materials you will need:
▶A sheet of stiff paper—about 15 cm square, a piece of wooden dowel or a thin stick about 30 cm long, a piece of stiff wire, and two small beads.

What to do:

1. Make five small holes in the square of paper at A, B, C, D, and E, and cut the paper along the dotted lines—as shown here.

2. Make a small hole in the piece of dowel—2 cm from the top end—and thread the wire through. One end of the wire is twisted around the dowel, the other should stick out at right-angles—like this.

3. Thread the beads and the square of paper on to the wire, in the following order:

First, one of the beads, then the paper at hole E.

Fold the four corners of the paper inwards and pass the wire through holes A, B, C, and D.

Lastly, thread on the remaining bead and twist the end of the wire into a loop to hold the four arms of the windmill in place.

That's it. Now it's ready to turn.

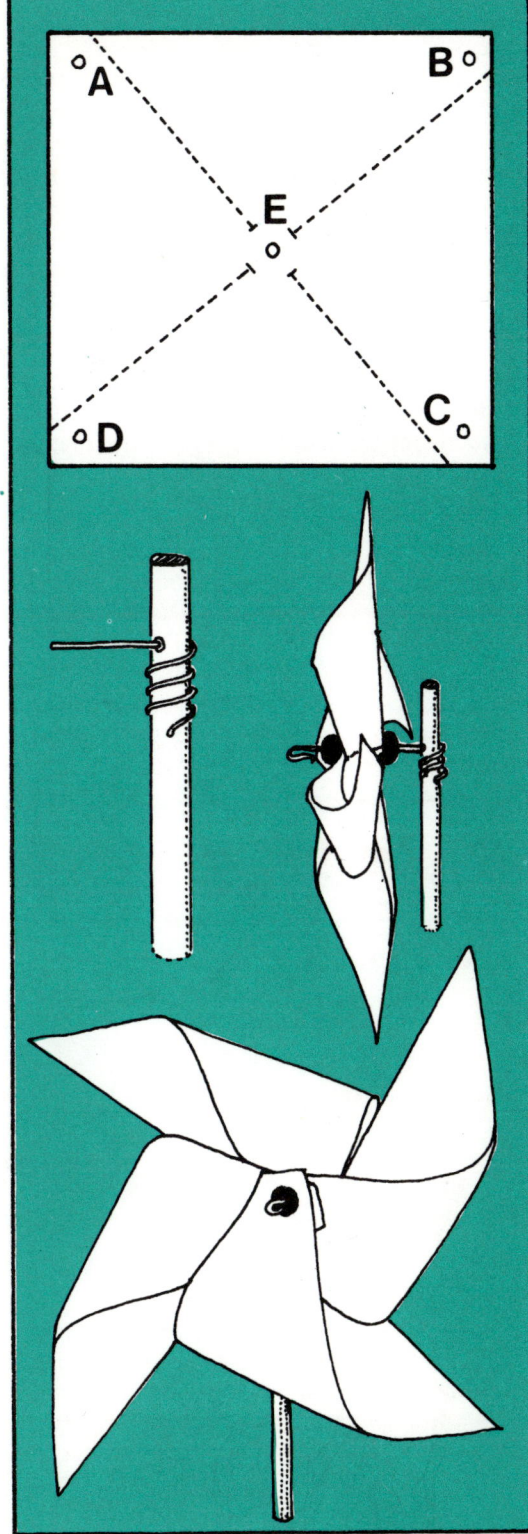

The Phenakistoscope
France

This was one of the early optical toys which gave rise to the cinema. It is, if you like, a very simple film, with twelve slightly different pictures, which, when seen by the eye in a split second, appear to be just one moving picture.

Joseph Antoine Ferdinand Plateau, a French scientist, invented it in 1832.

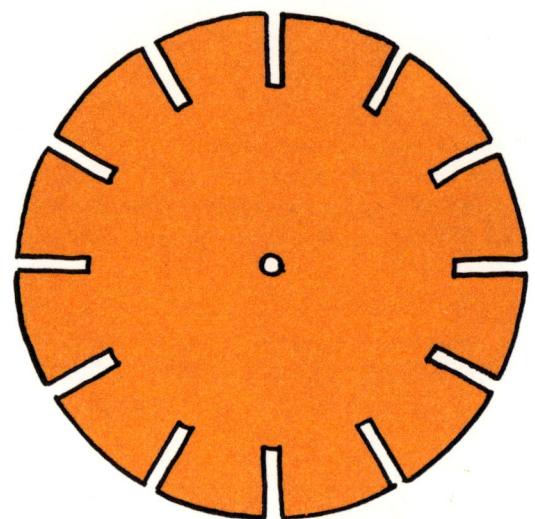

Materials you will need:
A circular piece of card about 20 cm diameter, a wooden clothes-peg, and a nail.

What to do:

1. Divide the piece of card into twelve equal segments, and cut out twelve thin slits. If the slits are too wide, the picture will be hazy. Using a 20 cm diameter circle, make the slits about $2\frac{1}{2}$ to 3 cm long and 2 mm wide.

2. In each of the spaces between the slits, draw a little picture or design, but make each picture slightly different, like this:

The drawings here will give you some ideas.

3. Fasten the disc (picture-side-out) on to the end of a clothes-peg (or any wooden stick) with a nail, so that the disc will spin quickly round when you flick it.

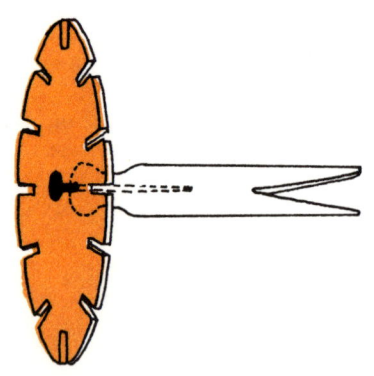

4. To see the moving picture, hold the disc in front of a well-lit-mirror—about a foot away; peer through one of the slits so that you can see the pictures reflected in the mirror, and spin the disc. Voilà—the picture comes to life.

Kite
China

Two thousand years ago, the great Chinese general, Han Hsin, had a problem—how to capture the palace which lay in his advance.

The palace was a strong one; well-guarded and well-provisioned, with ample stores of water and food. It was rich too, with silks and sandalwood, jewels and silver. But more than that, it was a strategic stronghold, well-placed with its hill position to command the vast plain which lay around it. Han Hsin longed to capture it. But how?

Neither his archers nor his fast-mounted cavalry had any effect. The palace seemed impenetrable.

Han Hsin sat in his tent and thought.

But he was tired—so tired that his mind wandered back to the pleasanter days of his childhood—to the days spent in the country, watching the farmers at work in the field. All of a sudden, he jumped up. The answer was there—in the fluttering rags which the farmers used to frighten the birds.

What if he were to fasten some rags to a thread, he thought, and fly them towards the palace? Then he could calculate the exact distance from his camp to the palace walls. And if he dug a tunnel, passing his most trusted swordsmen into the palace by night . . . the seige would be over. And that is what he did. Han Hsin dug the tunnel—captured the palace—and invented the first kite.

Materials you will need:

▶*Frame:* Two lengths of thin, wooden dowel, each about 60 cm long;

▶*Cover:* Thin strong paper (tissue paper or thin brown wrapping-paper) or plastic (thin polythene sheet), gummed paper tape, and strong twine;

▶*Line:* Thin string or nylon thread, and a simple reel.

What to do :

1. Notch each end of the dowel, like this.

2. Fasten the two pieces of dowel together to make a cross, by binding the join very tightly with strong twine.

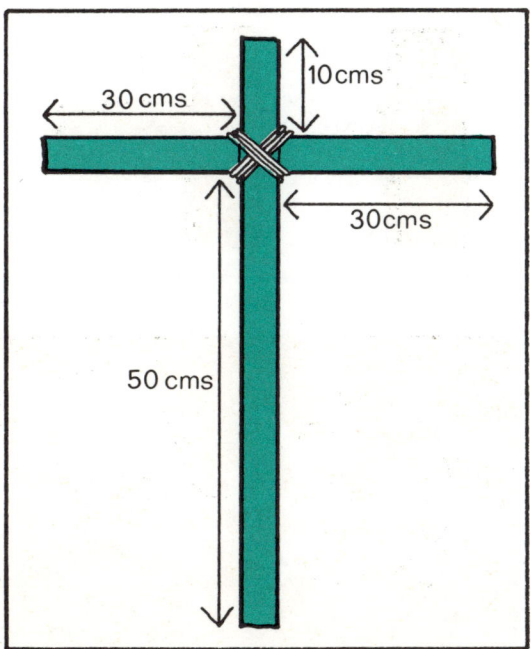

If you are using 60 cm lengths of dowel, the proportions of the cross should be as shown, and you must take great care to fasten the cross-piece exactly on the centre point to give correct balance.

10 cms

30 cms

30 cms

50 cms

3. Thread a length of string around the ends of the cross to make a taut frame.

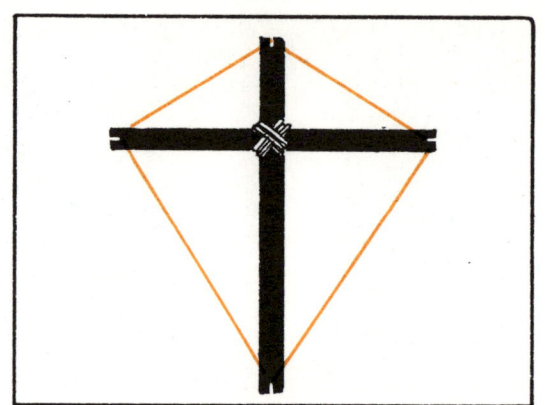

4. Cover the kite with paper or plastic.
Remember that the kite must be as light as possible, so use the thinnest and strongest paper or plastic that you can find. Cut the cover slightly bigger than the frame so that you can fold the edges over and fasten them down.

For a paper cover, use gummed paper tape.

For a plastic one, use transparent adhesive tape.

5. For the line, you will need about 100 metres of strong, thin string or, better still, a nylon fishing-line with a breaking strain of 5 kilos or more.

Wind the line on to a simple reel (something like this), and fasten the end to the kite cross-piece.

Now all you need is a fine day and a steady breeze.

Points to remember:

★ Keep the kite as light as possible. By and large, the lighter the kite, the higher it will fly.

★ If the kite bobs and weaves and dives too much, give it a short tail, using a length of string with strips of paper fastened at 20 cm intervals.

★ Never fly your kite in stormy weather, or near power lines.

Gingerbread Man
British Isles

Is a gingerbread man a toy or a biscuit? If it's a biscuit, it's also a very good toy. If it's a toy, then unlike most other toys, it's good to eat. Perhaps we can best think of it as an edible toy.

No one can say who first made a gingerbread man, but we do know that ginger has been used for thousands of years. The word 'ginger' comes from an old Indian word meaning horn stem, which describes very well the knobbly root of the ginger or zingiber plant from which ginger is made. And it was from these dried roots, carried across the seas from India and the Far East, that gingerbread men were first made in England, as toys or biscuits, to be sold on feast-days at country fairs.

To make about four or five gingerbread men you will need:
▶ ½ teacupful of self-raising flour
▶ 2 level tablespoons of sugar
▶ 1 ½ oz butter
▶ 1 level teaspoon of ground ginger
▶ a pinch of salt, an egg, and a few currants.

What to do (after first checking with your mother that you can use the oven):

1. Rub the butter and the flour together with your fingers in a large bowl—until the mixture is crumbly.
2. Add the sugar, ginger and salt, and stir the mixture together with a spoon.
3. Add the egg, and mix together to make a stiff paste.
4. Roll the mixture quite thin with a rolling-pin on a floured board.
5. Cut out the shapes of gingerbread men with a knife, adding currants for eyes, nose, mouth, and buttons.
6. Place the cut-out shapes on a piece of cooking foil, lightly smeared with cooking oil. Put the foil on a cooking tray, and put it into the oven (pre-heated to 350°F).

7. Cook the biscuits for about twenty minutes. Take them out of the oven and let them cool. If they look good enough to eat— eat them; if not, you have four or five long-lasting gingerbread people.

Punch
British Isles

Three hundred years ago in the village of Acerra in Italy, there lived a poor old farmer. His face was very red, his nose very big, and his name was Puccio d'Anielle.

His face was so red, and his nose so big that people laughed at him. He was very sad.

One day, a fair came to the village, with stalls and roundabouts and (most exciting of all) a puppet theatre. Everyone was there, jostling, laughing and shouting. And Puccio was there too, but he sat in a corner of the village square where no one could see him.

All of a sudden, Puccio heard a voice.

"What a marvellous face," said the voice. "What a wonderful nose."

Puccio looked up. The voice was coming from a very tall and a very important-looking man.

"Forgive me," said the man. "My name is Signor Fiorillo. I am the puppet master."

Signor Fiorillo sat down, and they talked.

It would take far too long to tell you all that was said; all we need to know is that Puccio was to become famous. He was to have a puppet named after him.

The first puppet which Signor Fiorillo made in honour of his friend was called Pulcinella, but as the years passed, the name slowly changed. Pulcinello—Puncinello—Punchinello. And when Punchinello arrived in London in 1662 he became known—quite simply—as Punch. How he met and married Judy, bought his dog, Toby, and fought with the wicked crocodile is another long story. But to begin with, this is how to make Punch.

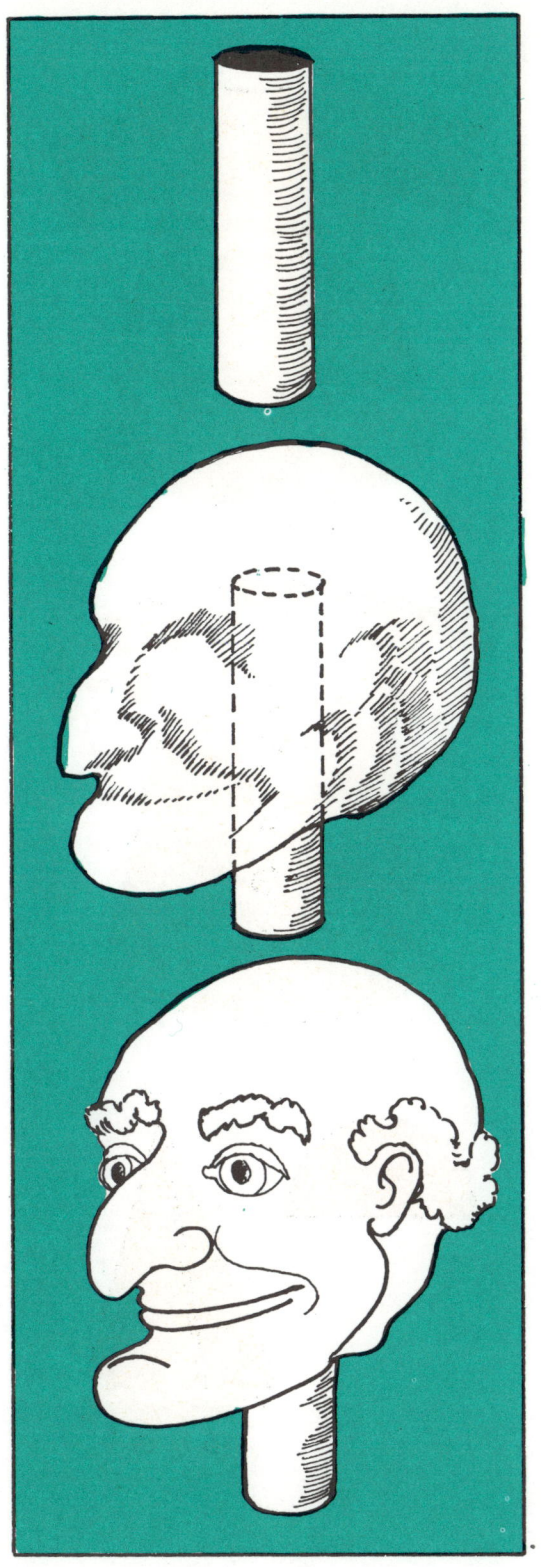

Materials you will need:

▶Papier-maché paste (see page 48), thin card, felt or coloured cloth, a few buttons, cotton wool, and some strips of ribbon lace.

What to do:

1. Make a small cardboard tube about as long as your index finger, and just wide enough to fit over it.

2. Take a small ball of papier-maché—about as big as a small apple—and model it carefully around the cardboard tube into the face of Punch.

3. Put the finished head to dry. In a warm room it will take about three days, but if you put the head into a warm oven (after asking your mother's permission) it will dry in a few hours.

4. When the head is completely dry it can be painted. Put a few wisps of cotton wool around the ears.

5. To makè Punch's dress, cut out two pieces of cloth—like the one shown here.

The neck hole should be just large enough to fit around the cardboard tube. The sleeves should be long enough to cover your thumb and forefinger; and the dress, long enough to cover your hand and part of your forearm.

Sew the pieces together around the edge —but not at the neck and sleeve openings, or along the bottom.

Turn the shape inside-out, and the dress is ready to receive collar, cuffs, and buttons. Collars and cuffs can be made by sewing a strip of ribbon lace around the edge.

6. Fasten the neck of the dress on to the neck of the head with PVA adhesive (see page 48), and allow it to dry.

7. For the pointed hat, cut out a semi-circle of felt, sew the two straight edges together, and finish off with a border of ribbon lace around the bottom.

8. Fasten the hat on the head with adhesive, and there you have it. Puccio d'Anielle lives again.

(You could make a puppet of Judy in the same way.)

22

FOLD

Kachina Doll
U.S.A.

A Kachina, so the Hopi Indians of Arizona believe, is a spirit, half-man and half-god. There are many of them. The Kachina of the sun, of the moon, the still water and the fast river, the moon and the stars.

Sometimes, the Kachinas live among the people in their villages; sometimes they depart to live alone in the high mountains.

Then, to remind the tribe of the departed Kachinas, ceremonial dances are performed by masked men, and parents make models, like the one shown here, in imitation of the Kachinas, to help their children remember the missing spirits.

Materials you will need:
▶A small block of soft wood, feathers, paints, a little glue, and a penknife.

What to do:

1. A Kachina doll is very simple to carve, since only a few details are required. Use a block of pine wood, or better still, soft balsa wood, from which to carve the shape.
2. Paint the carved shape, as you see here, using only a few poster paints—red, black, white, brown and yellow.
3. Add a few small, white feathers for the head-dress.

23

Daruma Doll
Japan

Long ago, in the Far East, there lived an old man. The Chinese called him Ta-mo—the Japanese, Ot-tok-I. Others called him Daruma, and some say that his real name was Bodhidharma, and that he came from India.

But whatever his name (I will call him Daruma, which is as good a name as any other), everyone agrees that he was a Buddhist priest.

For many years he travelled the land, teaching and praying and helping those less fortunate than himself, until one day, tired of his teaching and his travelling, he sat down to meditate.

And he sat, and sat and sat—and continued to sit. Not for a day, or a week, or a month, but for nine whole years.

And when at last he tried to get up, he couldn't—his legs had just withered away.

Whether it is true (as some people say) that he continued his travels by rolling along, no one knows, but everyone now thinks of him as a symbol of endurance and perseverance, and for that reason, the little doll which represents him (however much you try to push it over) can never be knocked down. Little Daruma always stands upright.

Materials you will need:

▶ A ball of Plasticine, newspaper, Polycell paste, PVA adhesive (see page 48) or adhesive tape, and a small pebble.

What to do:

1. Model the ball of Plasticine into a smooth, round-bottomed shape, like this. Make the shape as smooth as you can, and take great care to make the bottom perfectly rounded.

2. Dampen a sheet or two of newspaper, and tear it into postage stamp-sized pieces. Fasten the pieces all over the Plasticine shape with Polycell paste, and keep on doing so until you have made five or six complete layers.

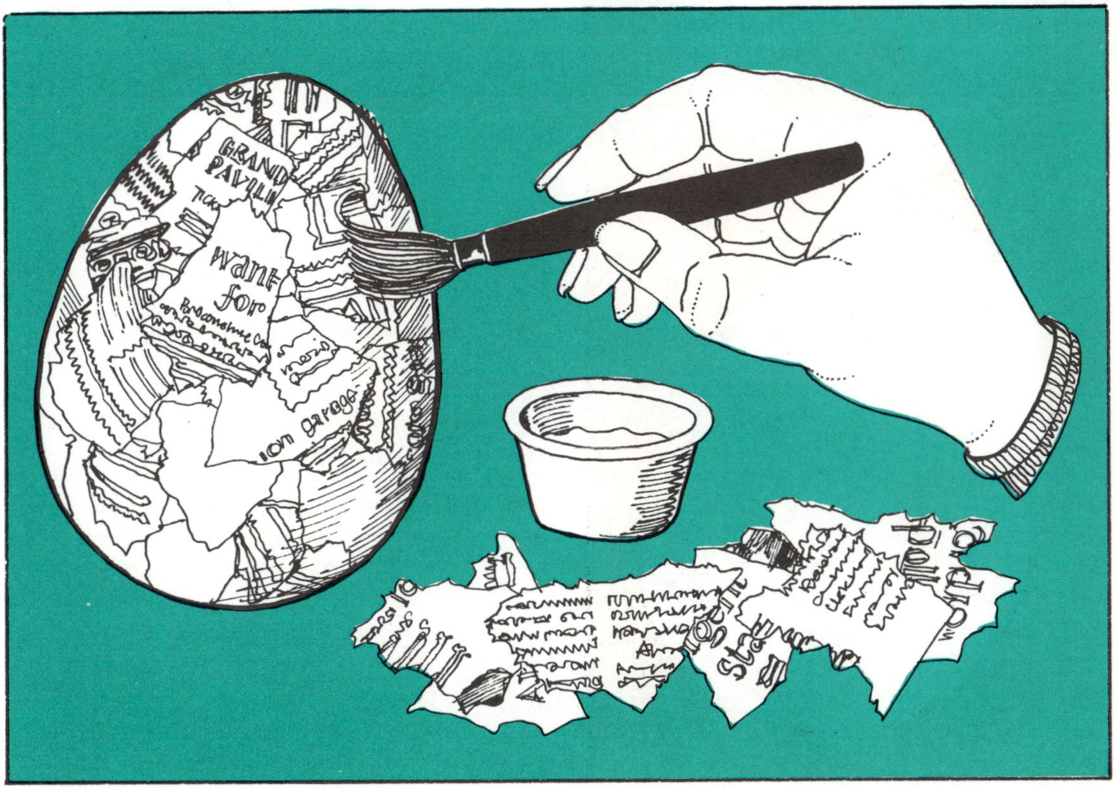

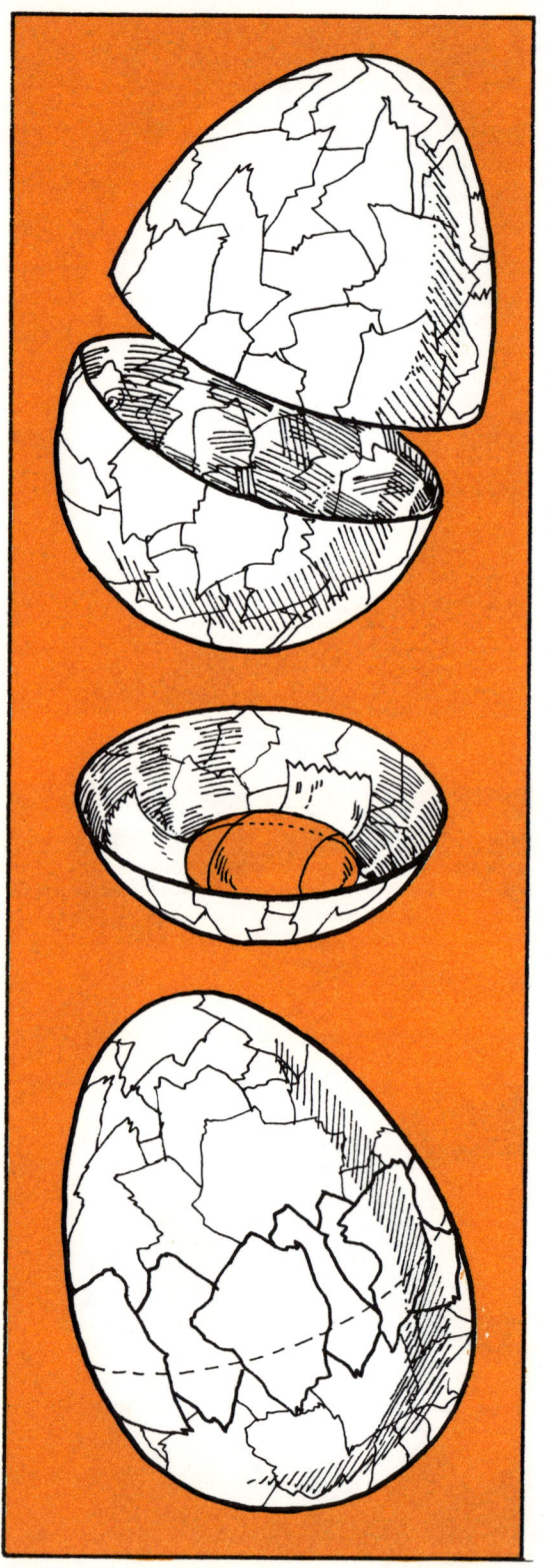

3. When the paper covering is completely dry, cut the shape in half and remove the Plasticine.

4. Fasten a small, heavy weight (a pebble will do) on to the inside of the bottom half with adhesive tape or PVA adhesive, making sure that it is very firmly secured.

5. Fasten the two halves together again with adhesive tape—or, better still, with more layers of newspaper and Polycell paste.

When the model is dry, it can be painted or coloured.

Of course, you can paint your Daruma doll in any way you wish, you might even give it a little dress or a hat, but ours are Japanese.

27

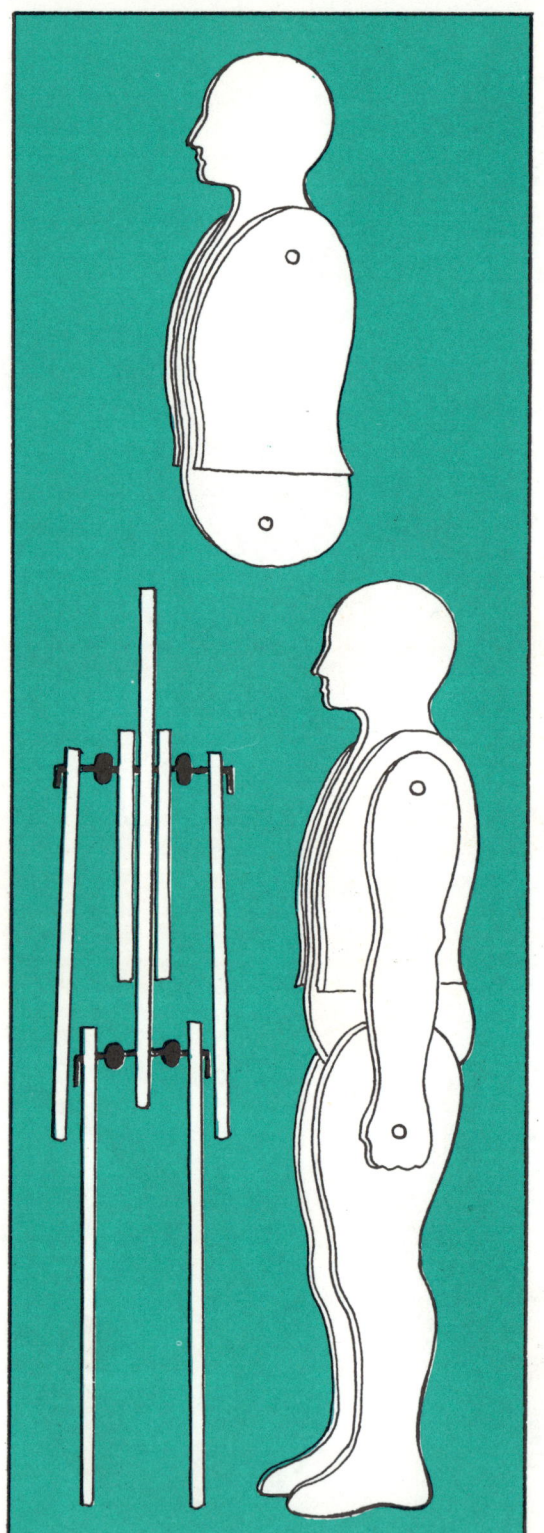

Acrobat
Germany

Materials you will need:
▶Thick card, a small block of wood and two wooden strips, a length of thin dowel, four beads, two corks, short strips of stiff wire, and PVA adhesive (see page 48).

What to do:

1. Cut out the shapes shown opposite from thick card. You will need two shapes like B, two like C, two like D, and one like A.

2. The hole at the bottom end of shape C should be just large enough to receive the length of dowel; all the other holes should be the size of a nail-head.

3. If you want to paint the model do it now, before the pieces are put together.

4. Fasten the two B shapes to the A shape with glue.

5. Now attach the arms and legs. Do this with a strip of stiff wire, bending the ends of the wire over to secure the pieces, with a bead at each shoulder and leg joint to separate them from the body—as you see in the section drawing.

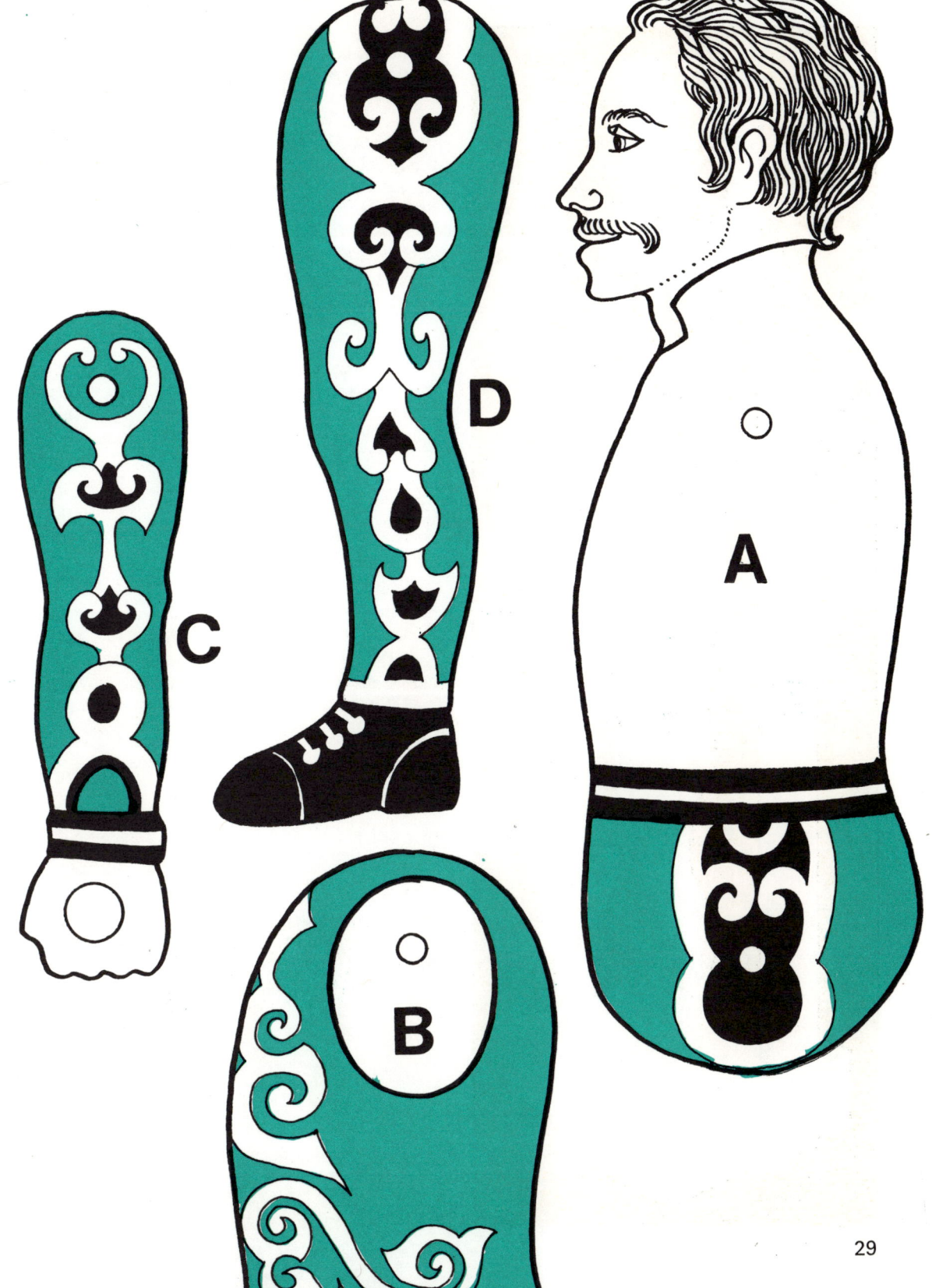

C

D

B

A

29

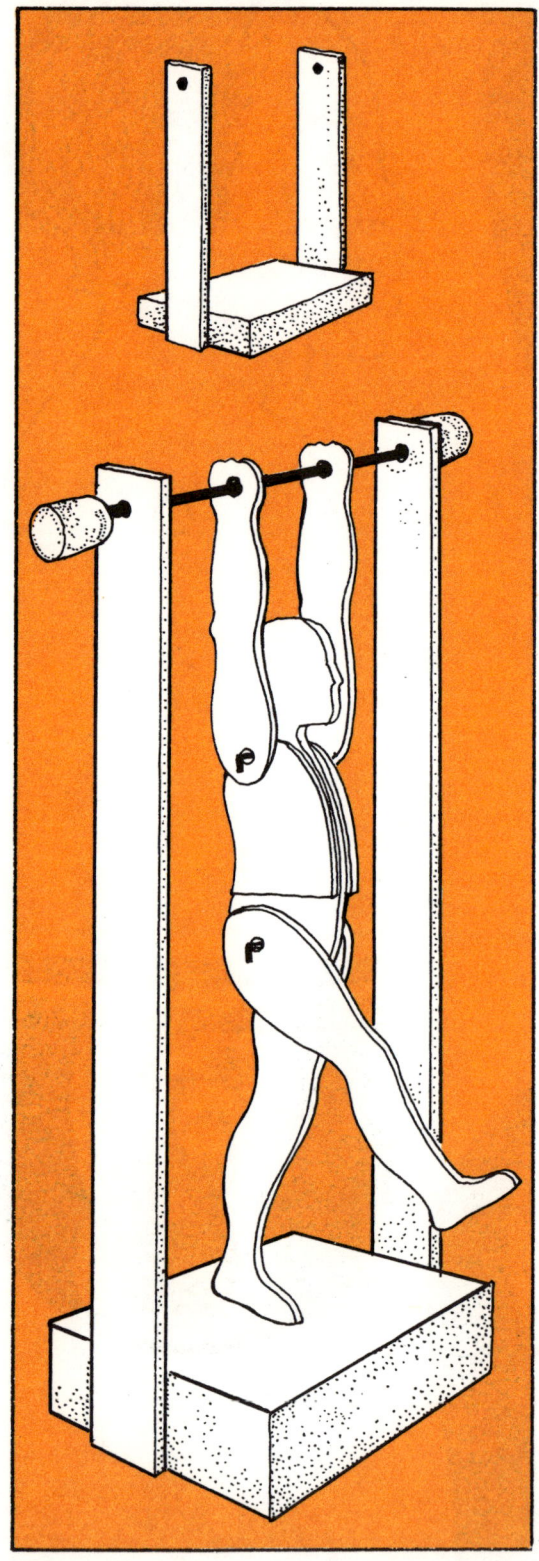

6. Take two pieces of wood strip (very thick cardboard can also be used) each piece being 33 cm long, about 3 cm wide, and 1 cm thick. At one end of each piece of wood, drill a hole slightly larger than the piece of dowel, 2 cm from the edge. Nail the undrilled ends to a block of wood about 10 cm by 6 cm by 3 cm—like this.

7. Take the thin length of dowel and thread it through the supporting stand and the up-raised arms of the acrobat, finishing off with a cork at either end—as you see here.

8. Lastly (and this is very important) put a spot of PVA adhesive on either side of the hands where they are attached to the dowel, and allow the adhesive to set before the model is used.

That's it. The model is finished. As you will have guessed, the acrobat is worked by twisting one of the corks, but if it seems to be stiff, check the joints at the arms and legs, and make the holes bigger, if necessary.

Pantin
France

No one really knows who invented the pantin or jumping jack, but it caused quite a sensation when it was introduced into France in 1746. Within a short time, everyone seemed to have one—boys and girls, shopkeepers, bakers—even Duchesses and politicians, until they caused such a commotion that the French police decided to ban them.

Materials you will need:
Some card, cotton, and four paper-fasteners.

What to do:

Cut out two arms (A and B), two legs (C and D), and a head and body (in one piece, G) from stiff card, and fasten them together with the four paper-fasteners, pushed through fairly large holes, like this:

Thread a loop of cotton from A to B, and a loop from C to D.

Tie a long piece of cotton at E and F, leaving a long tail; and a short piece of cotton at G.

By holding the cotton at the top, and pulling at the cotton at the bottom, jack will begin to jump.

(If the arms and legs seem a little stiff, remove the paper-fasteners and make the holes bigger.)

French pantins were made in all shapes and sizes—some to represent ballerinas others to represent soldiers. You might like to try making a 'footballer' pantin—or a spaceman—or anybody or anything at all.

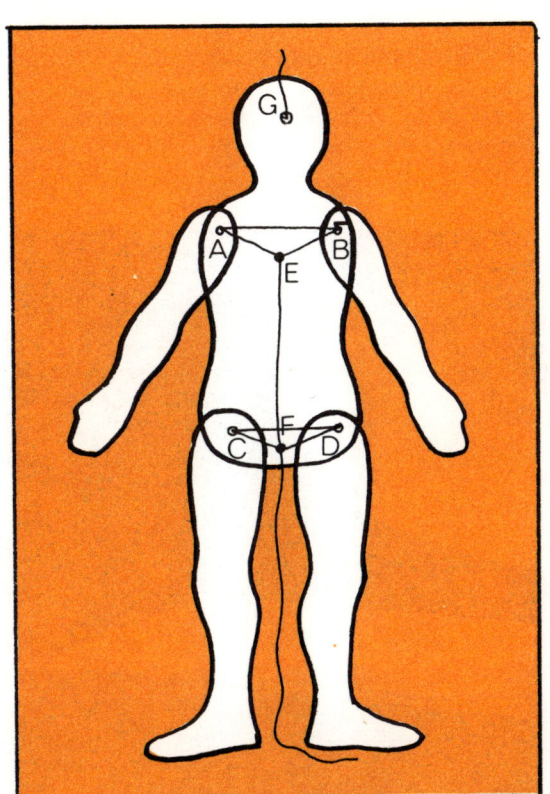

Pecking Bird
Poland

Materials you will need:

▶Thick cardboard, cotton thread, PVA adhesive (see page 48), a short piece of wire, a small, heavy weight, and a plastic bottle-top about 3 cm in diameter.

What to do:

1. Cut out the shapes which you see opposite from thick cardboard. You will need one shape A, one shape B, and two shapes like C. To make them as accurate as possible, take a tracing of them first.

2. Make holes in the cardboard shapes at points 1 to 6, exactly as they are shown opposite. Holes 2 and 4 can be quite small, the others should be slightly larger than a match head.

3. The next step will be to put the pieces together, but before you do, paint or decorate the pieces. Our pecking bird has a Polish design painted on it, but you may want to decorate yours differently.

4. Take the two C shapes—score them along the line **a-b**—and fold them along the score-line.

5. Fasten the two C shapes and the bottle-top on to shape A, in the positions marked opposite, with PVA adhesive. Now the model should look like this:

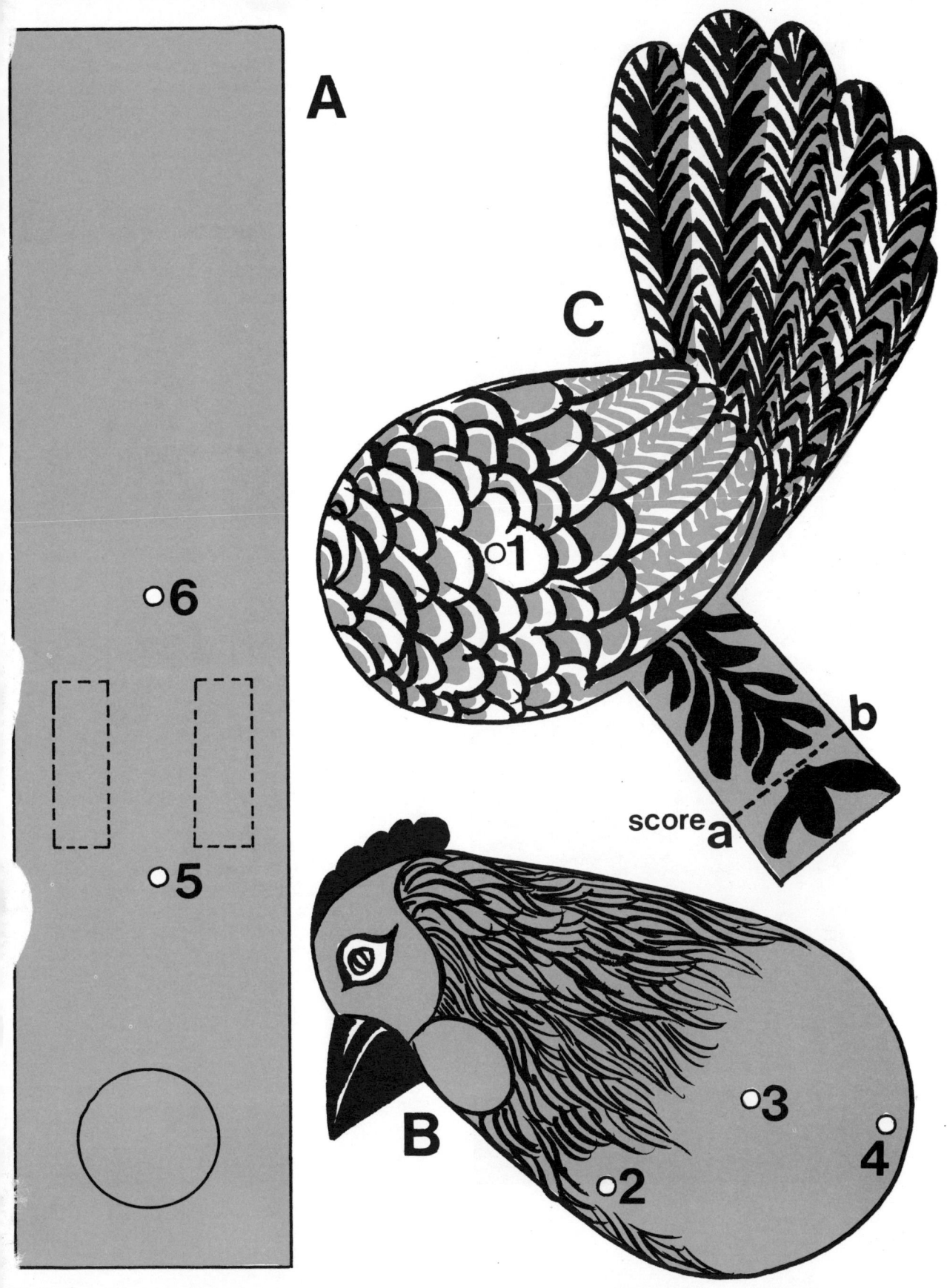

A

C

1

b

score a

B

2

3

4

5

6

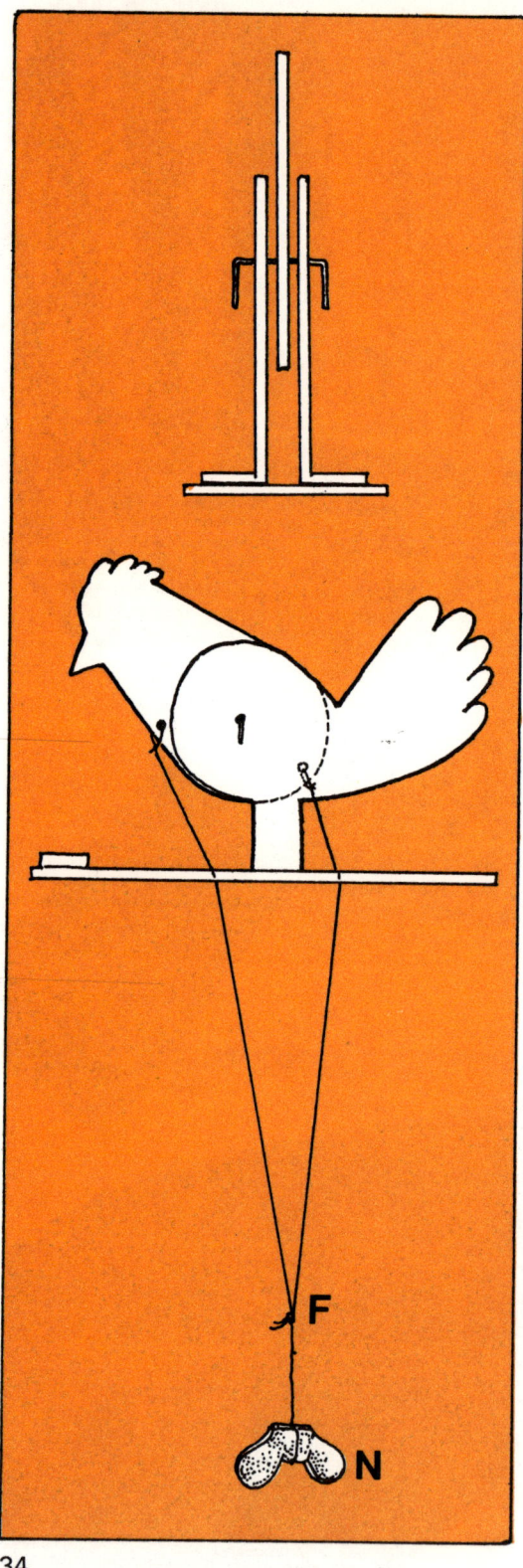

6. Tie pieces of cotton (each about 35 cm long) to the bird's head (shape B) at holes 2 and 4. Thread the cotton from hole 2 through hole 5, and the cotton from hole 4 through hole 6, of the base (shape A).

7. Bend the short piece of wire (about 3 cm long) into a flattened-out U-shape and use it to attach the head to the body shapes at 1 and 3.

8. Fasten the two lengths of cotton together at F, and tie a small heavy weight (a heavy screw nut will do) at N. The length of cotton from hole 2 to F, and from hole 4 to F, should be about the same.

Now the pecking bird is ready to peck. Hold it firmly at the tail of shape A—swing the heavy weight like a pendulum—and there you are.

If the bird doesn't peck properly, check that you have made all the holes in the right places; that the cotton has been threaded properly; and that the weight is heavy enough.

Traditional pecking birds are to be found in all shapes and sizes, and are usually carved from wood. Wooden ones, of course, are harder to make, but cardboard is almost as good, and with a little practice in learning where to make the four holes 2, 4, 5 and 6, you will be able to design lots of new bird shapes for yourself.

Bilboquet
France

Bilboquet is the French name for a cup and ball game which has been played for centuries.

We know for sure that King Henry III of France and his court played the game in the sixteenth century—with bilboquets made of finely carved wood or ivory; but much simpler bilboquets made from all kinds of materials have been found all over the world —from China and the South Seas, to Mexico and America.

You can see from the picture here, how the game is played—twirling the ball round on its length of cord and catching it in the cup—yet it takes lots of practice to be able to catch it every time.

Materials you will need:

▶A strip of wood about 30 cm by 5 cm by 1 cm, a strong plastic or cardboard tub, a hollow rubber ball (just large enough to fit into the tub), a length of cord about 40 cm long, paints and PVA adhesive (see page 48).

What to do:

1. Fasten the tub to the end of the piece of wood with PVA adhesive, and leave it to dry until the adhesive has firmly set.

2. Thread the string through the hollow rubber ball. Secure the ball end with a knot, and tie the other end to the centre of the length of wood.

3. Paint your bilboquet with a simple design—leave to dry—and now begin to practise.

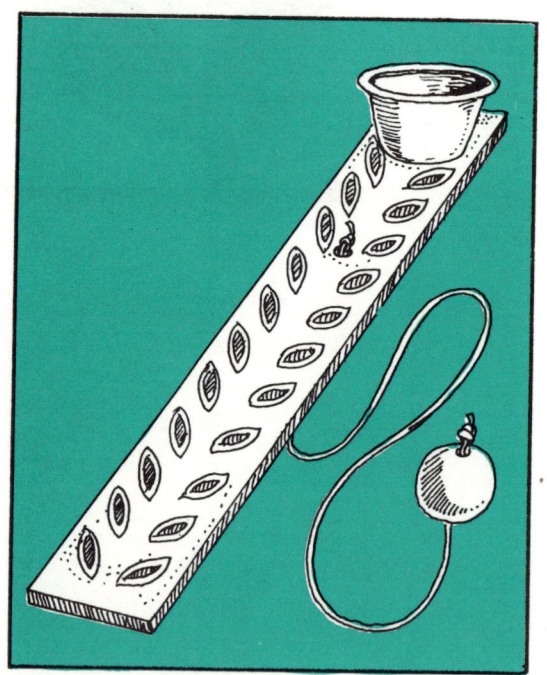

36

Clapper
Egypt

The clapper is a very ancient and a very simple noise-making instrument.

In Egypt it has been used for five thousand years or more; sometimes, quite simply, to frighten birds or locusts away from fields of corn; sometimes as an accompaniment to a dance; and sometimes in a ceremony of worship to Hathor, goddess of heaven, joy and death.

Materials you will need:
▶Two pieces of wood about 8 cm by 4 cm by 1 cm, one piece of wood about 18 cm by 4 cm by 1 cm, a short length of cord, and a drill.

What to do:

1. Drill two holes in each piece of wood at A and B.
2. Thread the cord through the holes, as you see here, and tie firmly together with a reef knot.

The noise is made by holding the clapper with the handle and shaking it, it's quite easy.

The top clapper shown here is a very plain one, but in the bottom one, the pieces of wood have been carved in the shape of hands, and decorated with symbols, which the early Egyptians may have used.

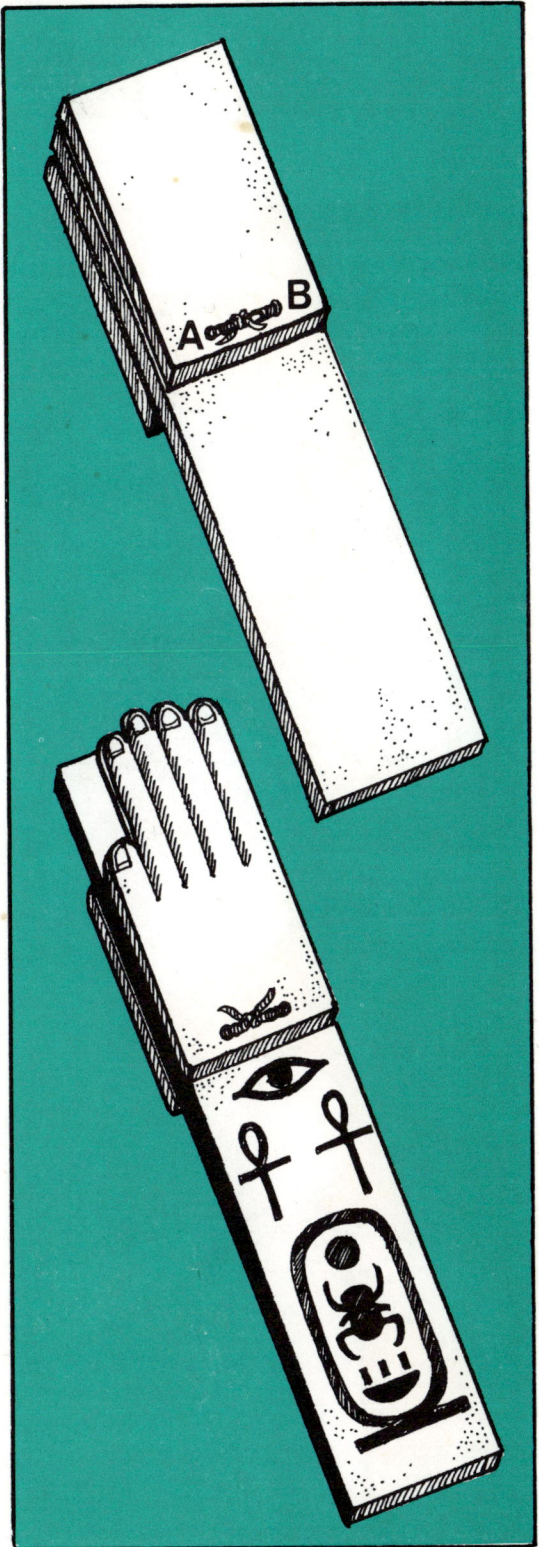

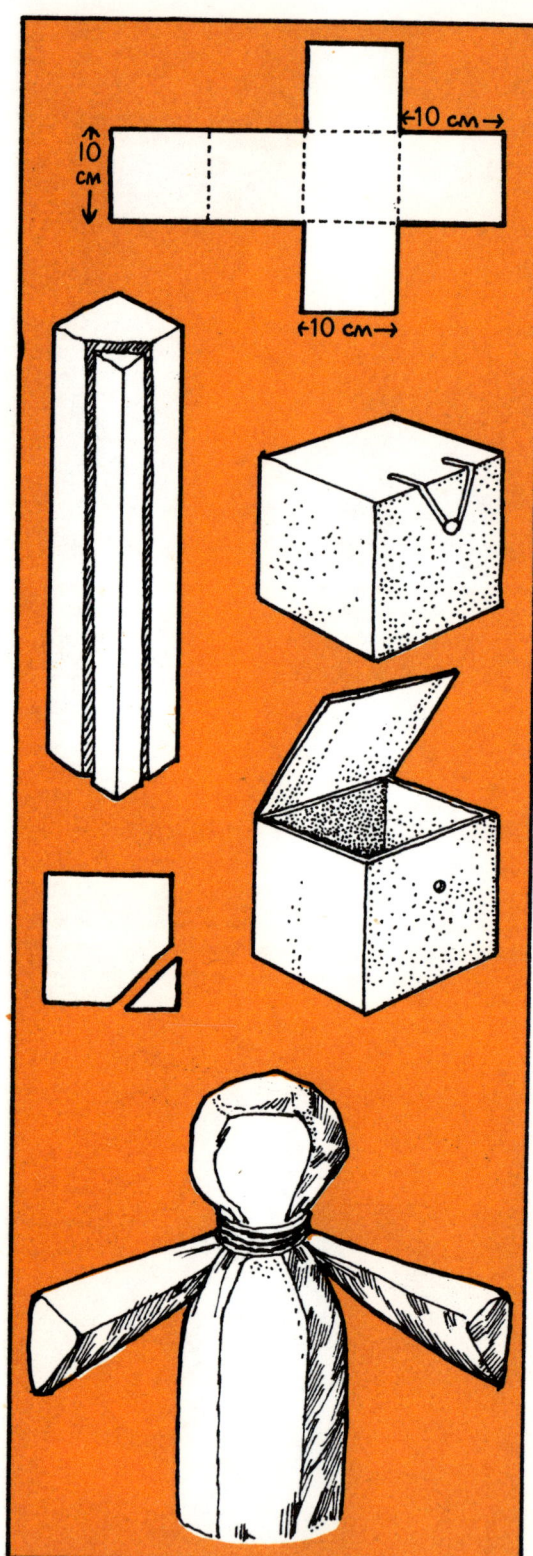

Jack-in-the-Box
France

Materials you will need:

▶A cardboard box with a lid, about 10 cm square, a length of foam rubber about 20 cm long by 5 cm square, string, a paper-fastener, pieces of felt, paint, and PVA Adhesive (see page 48).

What to do:

1. You may be able to find a ready-made box about 10 cm square, but if not, make one from a piece of stiff cardboard.

   Cut out the shape, as shown here—score along the dotted lines—fold up the sides, and tape the edges together with strong adhesive tape.

   Decorate the outside of the box with paints or cut-out gummed paper shapes.

2 Make a fastener for the box using a small loop of string threaded through two holes made in the lid, and a paper-fastener pushed into the front—as you see here.

3. Cut the foam rubber lengthwise and fasten the two lengths together with a piece of string—as in the bottom drawing—to make Jack's arms, head and body.

   Trim the head with a pair of scissors to make a nicely rounded shape.

4. Paint the figure with thick poster colour to make it look as frightening as possible. If you find paint difficult to use, decorate the figure with cut-out pieces of felt, fastened on with strong glue. You might even give the figure a felt hat, cotton-wool hair, felt hands, or a simple dress made from thin, patterned cloth, or the top of an old stocking.

5. Fasten the base of the figure to the inside base of the box with strong glue, and leave to dry until the glue has firmly set.

   Now all you have to do is to push Jack down into the box, close the lid, and wait for an unsuspecting friend.

Thumb Piano
Africa

In Africa, thumb pianos are made in all kinds of ways, from all kinds of materials, and in all shapes and sizes depending upon their country of origin.

In Uganda they are called sansas; in Nigeria—agidibos; and in Tanzania—lukembes. And they have lots of other names too. But we will call them thumb pianos, and this is how to make one.

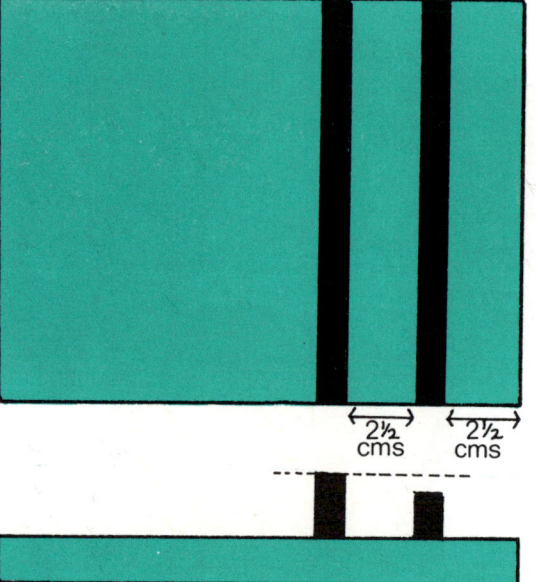

Materials you will need:
▶one block of wood 18 cm by 12 cm by 1 or 2 cm;
▶two strips of wood, each 12 cm by 1 cm by 1 cm;
▶one strip of wood, 12 cm by 2 cm by 1 cm;
▶a short piece of cane (an old garden cane will do) or bamboo;
▶two screws and a few nails.

What to do:

1. Shave or sandpaper down one of the 1 cm square strips to make it slightly thinner, and nail this strip and the remaining 1 cm square strip to the wooden base.

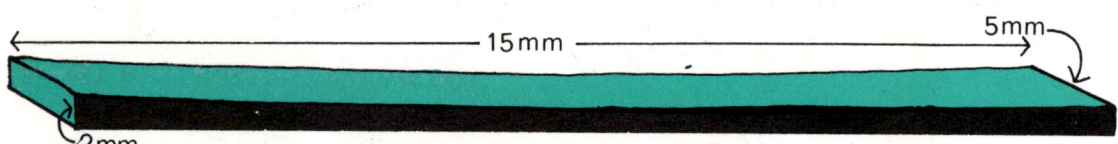

2. Cut eight thin strips from the piece of cane. Each strip should be 15 cm long, 5 mm wide, and 2 mm thick. The width and the thickness of the strips is very important, so cut the strips carefully, and smooth them with sandpaper.

To give you some idea of the proportions, the width of each strip should equal the width of two wooden matchsticks laid side by side. The thickness should be slightly less than the thickness of one wooden matchstick; and the thickness in the middle of each strip should be slighly less than the thickness at the end.

40

3. Hold the eight strips in place by screwing the remaining strip of wood to the base, placing the screws in any of the spaces between the bamboo strips.

4. The note which each strip will give depends on its length and thickness. Long strips give a low note; short ones, a high one.

Experiment first of all with long and short strips, to see how many different notes you can make. You might just decide to choose eight pleasing notes—with high and low notes jumbled together higgledy-piggledy; but if you want to make an octave scale— the 'doh, ray, me' kind of scale which you may have learned at school—here's what to do:

Place the left hand strip about 2 cm from the bottom edge of the base, making the other seven strips progressively shorter, until the right hand strip is about 4 cm from the bottom edge, as you see here.

Any fine tuning can be done by gently tapping in or pulling out the secured end of the strip.

5. To play the instrument hold the board with the fingers of both hands—the free ends of cane pointing towards you—and press down the strips with your thumbs, releasing them sharply to obtain the note.

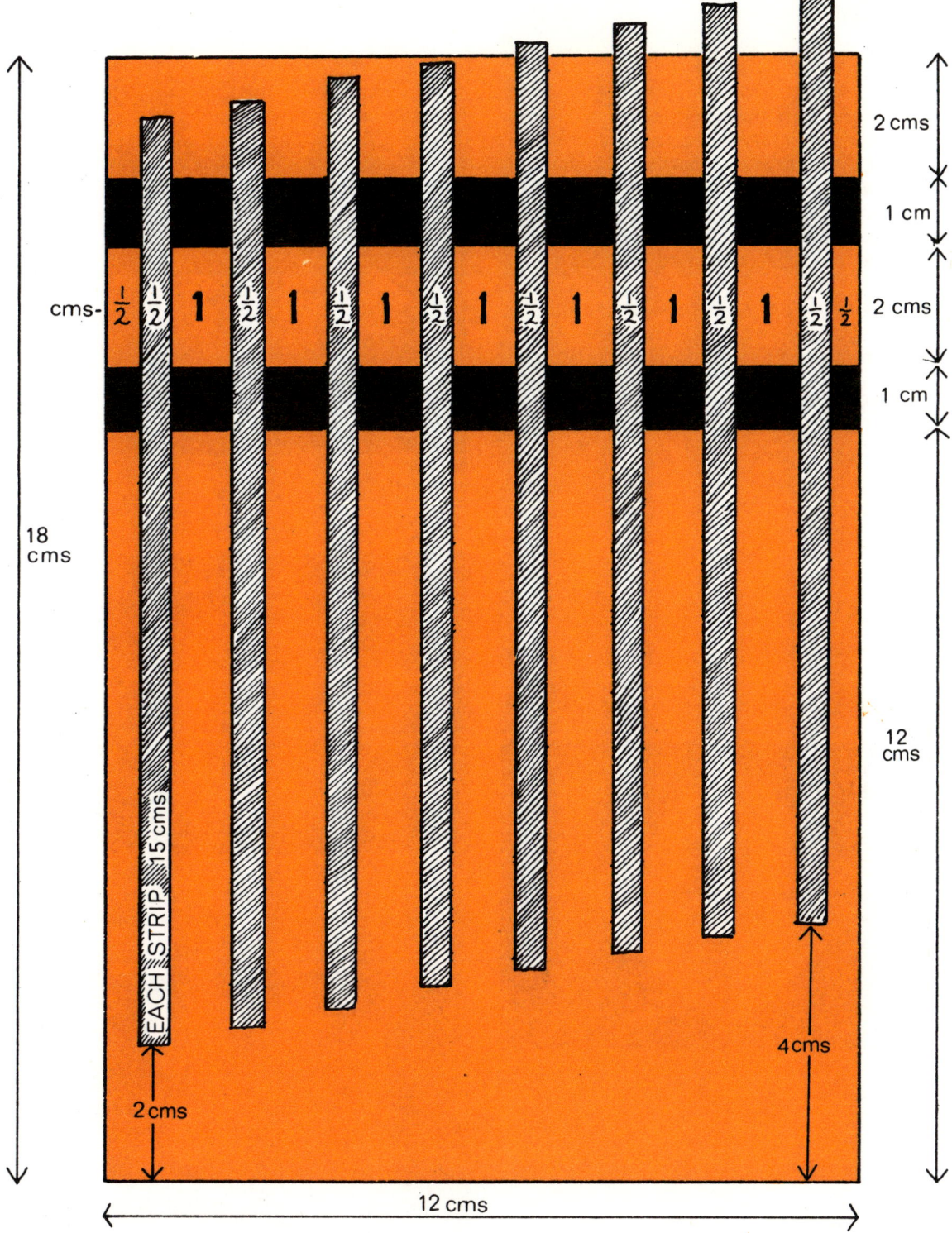

Origami Bird
Japan

Origami is paper-folding. Most of you will have done something like it before, when you made a folded-paper hat, or a paper boat, but traditional Japanese origami has four strict rules.

Whatever is to be made must be made from one square of paper, no cutting is allowed, nothing can be added, and nothing taken away.

Anyone can make a paper bird by cutting a piece here, and adding a piece there, but it's very difficult when you have to keep to the rules.

To make the bird, you will need a sheet of thin, strong paper about 20 cm square (notepaper is very good), and very nimble fingers.

What to do:

1. Fold the paper inwards along the dotted lines. Unfold it again and turn the paper over.

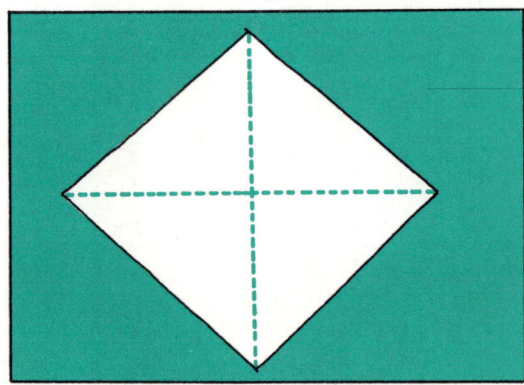

2. Again, fold the paper inwards along the dotted lines, and unfold it.

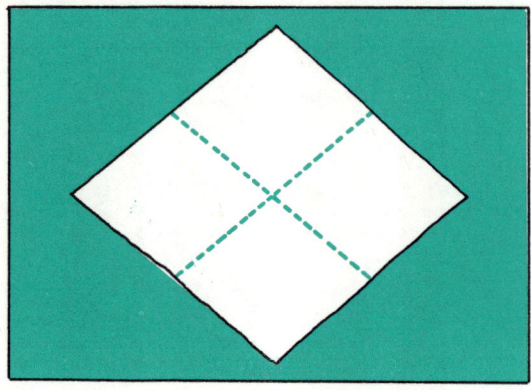

3. The paper should now look like this.

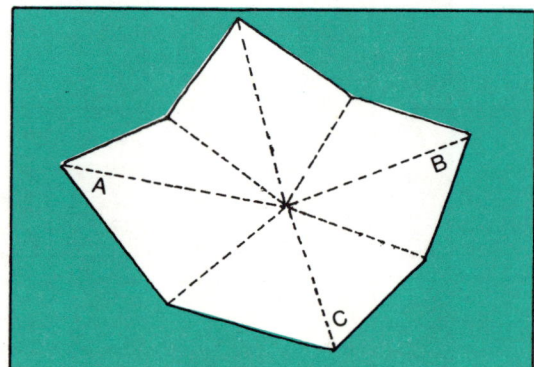

4. Bring the corners A and B together to meet at C.

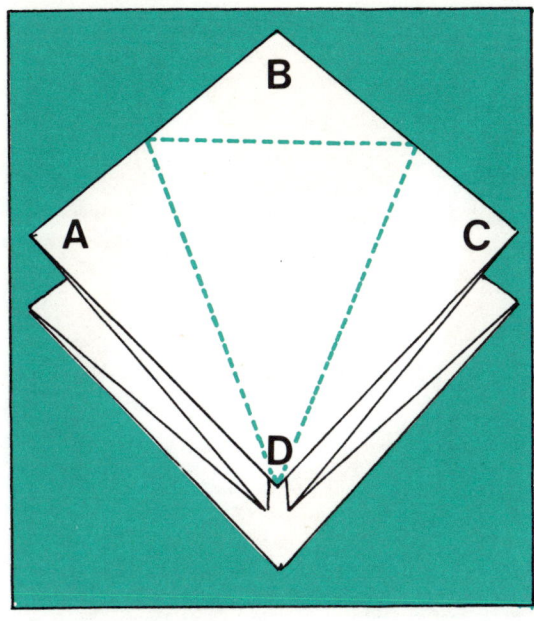

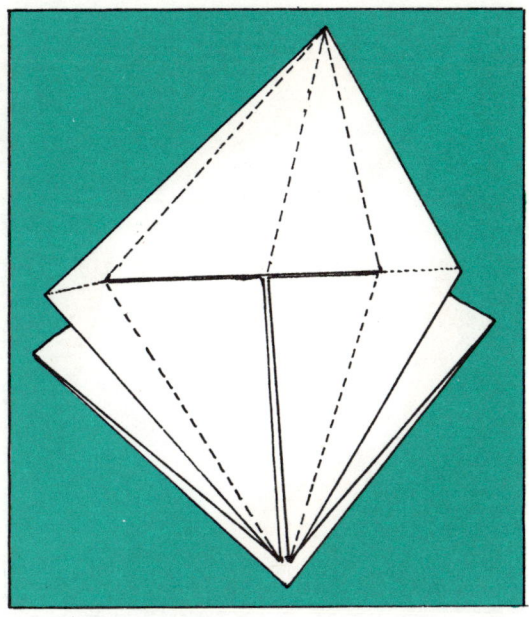

5. Fold the corners A, B and C inwards along the dotted lines, and unfold again.

Take the top layer of corner D, folding it up and over.

and press it down so that the paper looks like this.

6. Turn the paper over and repeat stage 5. Now your paper should look like this—

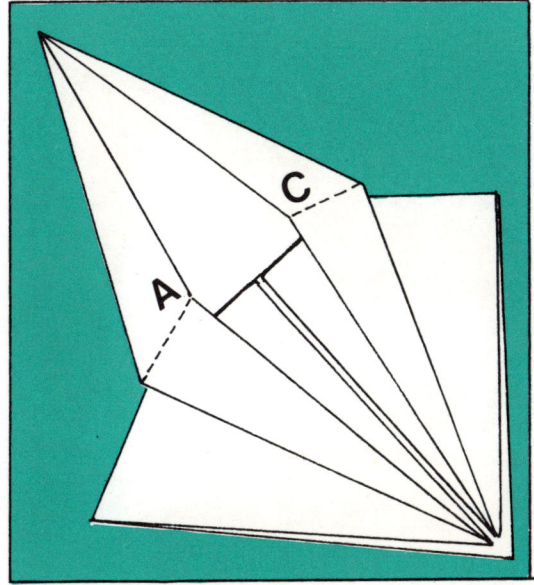

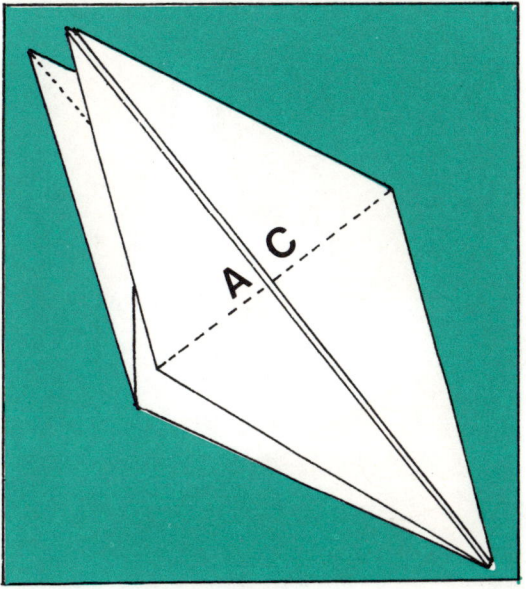

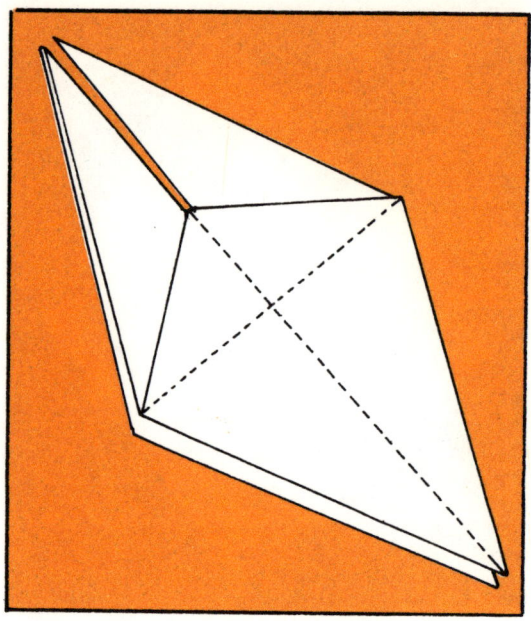

Fold the top layer of paper on side A over to side C.

Turn the paper over and do the same again.

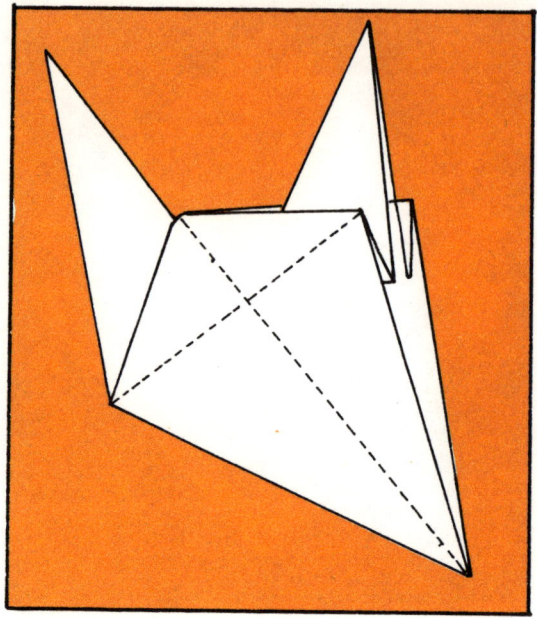

7. Holding the paper in the centre, pull down the top right-hand corner and press down.

8. Now do the same again with the left-hand corner, making a small fold for the head of the bird.

9. Fold the top layer of piece A upwards along the dotted line. Turn the paper over and repeat.

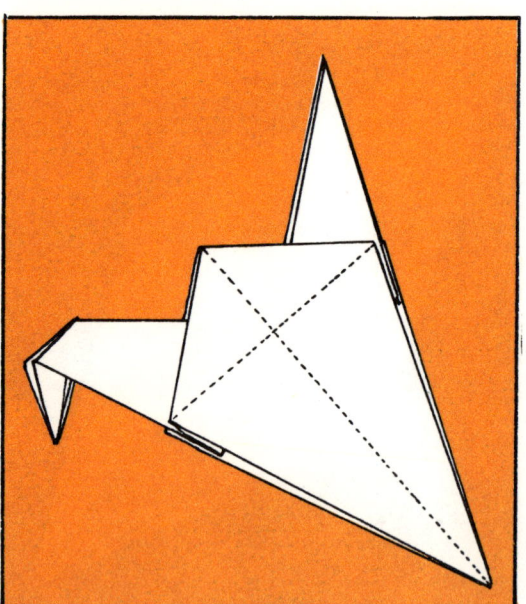

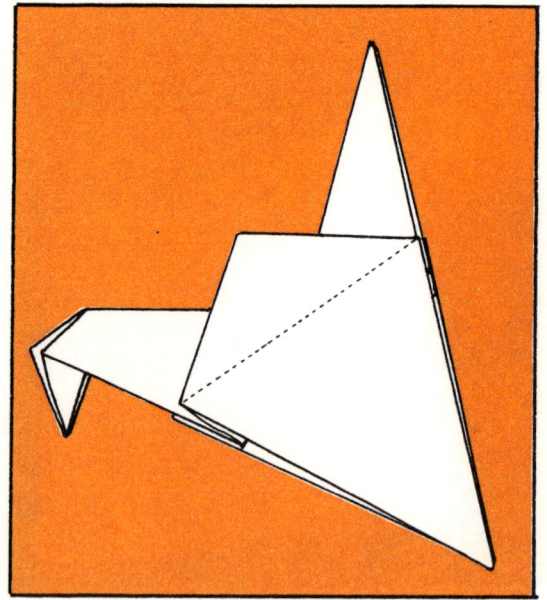

10. Fold the top layer downwards along the dotted line and unfold. Turn the paper over and do the same again.

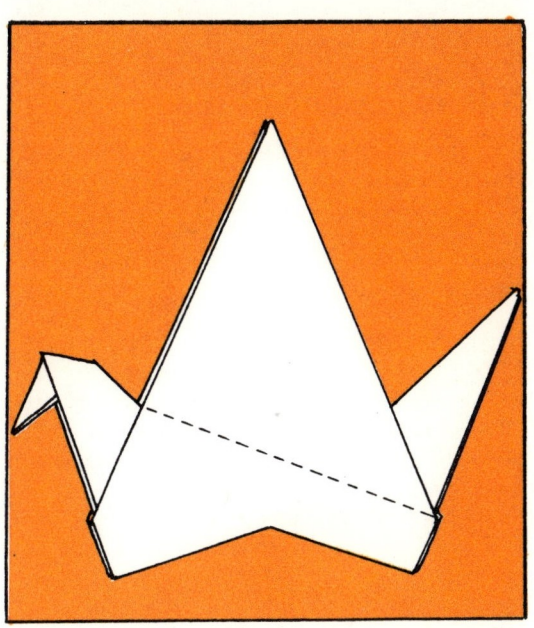

That's it. To make the bird flap its wings, hold it firmly at the front with one hand, and push the tail in and out with the other.

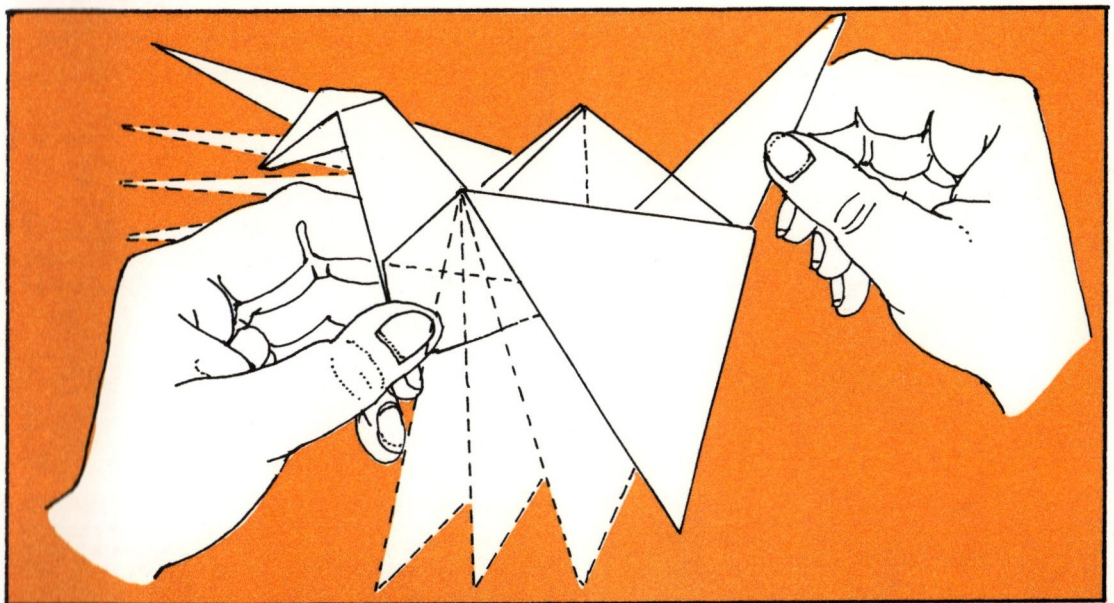

Materials

Adhesives and glues

For many of the toys described in this book you will need a strong glue to fasten the pieces together. But model-making shops and hardware stores sell so many different kinds—in jars, tins and tubes—that it's often difficult to know which to choose.

I suggest that you buy a PVA type adhesive (PVA is short for polyvinyl acetate). The letters PVA don't always appear on the label—manufacturers often give it a simpler name—so be sure to ask the shopkeeper for PVA.

It's thick, like treacle, but very white, and will stick almost anything. More important perhaps—if you spill it, or use a paint brush to apply it, it ·can be quite easily washed away with cold water. Yet when it dries hard, it is waterproof and transparent.

By mixing it with water (roughly half water and half PVA), you can make a varnish which can be painted over any of the toys described here, to give them a shiny finish, and help keep them clean.

Modelling paste for the Greek doll:
Instead of using ordinary modelling clay (which, as you know, has to be fired in a kiln to make it go hard) buy a packet of modelling paste from your local art or craft shop. Modelling paste looks like clay, and feels like clay, but it has something added to it which makes it set very hard without being fired in a kiln.

Some modelling pastes will set hard after being left on the window-sill for a day or so; others will require baking in the oven—but at a very low heat.

You can buy the paste in small polythene packets—it's quite cheap—and the printed instructions will tell you exactly how to use it.

Papier-maché paste for the Punch and Judy puppets:

1. Tear up two or three newspapers into very small pieces, and leave them to soak in half a bucketful of warm water with a tea-spoonful of washing-up liquid, for about a week.

2. Take out the paper pulp, squeezing as much water as possible from it with your hands, and put the squeezed-out pieces into a bowl.

3. Break up the pieces into tiny granules and stir in a cupful of flour and a cupful of thickly mixed wallpaper paste.

4. Knead the mixture with your hands until it is like soft clay. If the mixture is too wet, add some more flour; if too dry, add a little water. Now the papier-maché is ready to use.